$3.50

Other Books by W. Phillip Keller

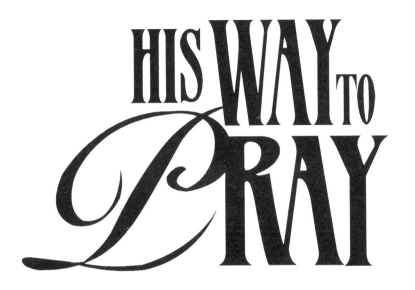

HIS WAY TO PRAY

A Devotional Study of Prayer

W. PHILLIP KELLER

kregel
PUBLICATIONS

Grand Rapids, MI 49501

His Way to Pray: A Devotional Study of Prayer

Copyright © 1997 by W. Phillip Keller

Published by Kregel Publications, a division of Kregel, Inc., P.O. Box 2607, Grand Rapids, MI 49501. Kregel Publications provides trusted, biblical publications for Christian growth and service. Your comments and suggestions are valued.

Cover design: PAZ Design Group
Book design: Nicholas G. Richardson

Library of Congress Cataloging-in-Publication Data
Keller, W. Phillip.
  His way to pray: a devotional study of the prayer life of Jesus / W. Phillip Keller.
     p.   cm.
  1. Jesus Christ—Prayers. 2. Jesus Christ—Devotional literature. I. Title.
BV229.K45   1997   248.3'2—dc20   96-34199
                                               CIP

ISBN 0-8254-2993-5

Printed in the United States of America
1 2 3 4 5 / 01 00 99 98 97

To those sincere churches of diverse denominations
who invited me to share these practical thoughts
on prayer with their people

Contents

Notes of Gratitude

It has been astonishing to see the keen response of so many to the simple studies on prayer that are the basis for this book. Our Father is calling Christians to seek His presence in honest prayer. (This must happen all over the Western world if our civilization is to be spared from utter ruin.)

I am deeply and humbly grateful to those churches who opened their doors and their lives to receive the call of Christ. It was especially encouraging to see many young men accept the truth from God's gracious Spirit.

There is also a note of thanks due to those friends who were so kind to drive my wife and me back and forth from these studies, especially after the awful automobile accident, which could easily have claimed my life. In His mercy and grace our Father has completely restored my capacity to drive again.

Again my genuine gratitude goes out to Fern Webber for turning a handwritten manuscript into a completed work ready for the publishers. She is always so eager, so efficient, and so excellent in her work! Blessings on her.

Finally let me say "thank you" publicly to my wife, Ursula, for her patience and understanding of my unusual work habits! Sometimes I start work at 2:00 A.M. while all the world is still.

To this I also add my appreciation to all those gentle, kind people who are constrained by Christ to pray for this rough old mountain man. Thank you!

About This Book

For the first fifty years of my life, even when I was far from truly knowing God, I stood in awe and quiet wonder at the manner in which He saw fit to answer the prayers of His people. The calm, unshakable confidence shown by some of His followers in His faithfulness to respond to their pleas aroused my utmost admiration. Obviously our Father was well aware of all that impacted the lives of those who trusted Him, and He took delight in rewarding their earnest requests.

But my personal problem, as it is with so many, was that I simply did not know the way to pray. Oh, from my earliest memories my parents and other kindly mentors had prayed with me, for me, around me. But at best *my* petitions were really quite pathetic and more or less perfunctory—done merely out of a sense of duty.

The terrible tragedy in all this empty exercise was that it astonished me to see the magnificent manner in which Christ honored the prayers of some humble souls, while more haughty people, like me, simply were bypassed. I wondered why. Looking back, I marvel at the mercy, patience, and gentle perseverance of God's gracious Spirit in teaching me how to pray in honesty.

From the foregoing the reader should not assume that I claim to be an authority on prayer. I do not! It is far too majestic an honor, too mysterious in its mighty power in the hand of the Most High, to be fully comprehended by a common person. Nor do I regard myself in any way as a great person of prayer. Quite the opposite! But I am grateful to say that year by year Christ is teaching me how to trust Him more.

He is the Great Rewarder of those who seek Him!

In the pages that follow, an earnest attempt is made to explain the seven basic forms of prayer most essential for honoring our Father. These are the private, innermost interactions between God and individuals. They deal with the inner sanctum of the soul. They show the way into the very presence of the Most High. The very essence of earnest prayer is an acute awareness of being in God's presence.

What transpires there determines the extent to which He is honored, and we in turn are assured of being heard. The hour of prayer is no longer a penance but a powerful, precious encounter with the Beloved. We call it the "hour of prayer" when it may be only the intensity of a few moments of utter stillness or long nights of prolonged intercession. It matters not the exact mode or manner. It is the *living* encounter with the *living* God that counts.

This little book does not deal with public prayer, liturgical prayer, corporate prayer, or other forms of communal prayer. It is at heart an honest endeavor to lead the reader into close communion with our Father. It is intended to help people come to the living Lord

Jesus Christ with the confidence one has in coming to a faithful Friend. It is to give searching souls an amazing assurance of God's gracious Spirit assisting them in their praying.

My earnest prayer is that, because of this work, many, many will move into a magnificent, fresh life of intense interaction with God. They will discover firsthand that He is one who honors the prayers of His people. He can change people; He can change their world. He is here, all is well! Be of good cheer!

1

The Prayer of Faith in God

It is very helpful, in fact most important, for us to understand why people pray. All sorts of societies and cultures for thousands of years, scattered all over the earth, have attached special importance to prayer in one form or another. Why, then, do we have an innate desire to pray?

Contrary to what most of us imagine, prayer did not originate with us, but it began with God Himself. In essence it is an action in the souls of human beings, ordained by our Father to enable us, His children, to commune with Him in harmony and great good will.

To fully grasp His enormous generosity in this gesture we need to go back into the earliest epoch of time. We need to see clearly something of His noble intentions, which are an essential expression of His supernatural character. We need to understand His profound love, which motivates all of His interaction with us.

His unique self-disclosure, given to us so freely in His Word, reveals that His very being is one of utter love. His

15

caliber of love is not a soft, sweet, sentimental emotion that people so often consider to be love. Rather, His love is a generous, gracious, grand action of His will to give—give and give freely to others of Himself and of His remarkable resources. This is the very goodness of God!

Out of this supernatural self-giving and self-sharing, there flows His divine desire to have children with whom He can share His very life. He dotes over us with unfailing compassion and infinite mercy, drawing us to Himself with loving care. He delights to draw near to us so that we, in response to His presence, can commune with Him, enjoy Him, trust Him. This is prayer!

This close, intimate communion is one of the noble and lofty honors that our Father bestows on us. Through the generosity of His own grace—expressed to us so fully in the perfect birth of His beloved Son, Jesus the Christ, coming to us as a child—we in turn now can come to Him as His children. All of this is made possible by the virtue of His perfect life, His perfect death, His perfect propitiation for us, His perfect resurrection in mighty power, His perfect ascension to the position of Supreme Intercessor on our behalf.

We no longer need to come to God our Father by way of animal sacrifices, complex religious rituals, some sort of lengthy liturgy, or even a special priesthood! Rather, in His amazing and beautiful generosity, God invites us to come directly into His presence by way of His own dear Son. He Himself put it to us so simply when He stated before His death in our stead: "I am the way, the truth, and the life: no man cometh unto the Father, but by me" (John 14:6).

It is upon this beautiful basis that it is possible for people to come freely, gladly, boldly into the supreme presence of our Father as His beloved children. We are given the joyous privilege to approach Him in childlike confidence anytime, anywhere, without apprehension, all because of the profound provision Christ Himself has made for us to pray in this intimate way.

Added to all of this, His Holy Spirit confirms within us that God is our Father. He assures us that Christ is our Friend, our Intercessor. In our praying, He, God's Spirit, also intercedes on our behalf, making our prayers pleasing and acceptable to God.

> And when thou prayest, thou shalt not be as the hypocrites are: for they love to pray standing in the synagogues and in the corners of the streets. . . . When thou prayest, enter into thy closet, and when thou hast shut thy door, pray to thy Father which is in secret; and thy Father which seeth in secret shall reward thee openly. But when ye pray, use not vain repetitions, as the heathen do: for they think that they shall be heard for their much speaking (Matt. 6:5–7).

Christ instructs not only the followers of His day but all of us today in the way to pray. We need to carry out His clear commands with great earnestness. They convey to us how to pray in forthright faith, quietly confident that our Father will respond to and openly reward our petitions.

First He advises us not to make a superficial, public display of our praying. This was and still is very much a common practice. Praying anywhere in public view is considered very pious, perfectly proper, and appropriate social and religious behavior. It attracts attention to the person who is praying. It is often done with the attitude of special piety.

But Christ calls us to a different sort of prayer—private prayer. It is at the very heart of a close communion, an interchange within the sanctum of our own souls, between us and God our Father.

He calls us to enter into the closet and close the door for an intimate encounter with our Lord. Across the centuries the church has often taught people that this meeting with God must be in some private place prepared as a rendezvous for prayer. This idea has merit for those who truly desire to be alone with God. But Christ was so much amongst the common people, He knew full well from His own life as a carpenter that ordinary men and women did not have elaborate homes with hidden closets or secret hideaways. At best, most of them lived in humble open rooms in full view of the family.

Where then is the secret spot of which He speaks? It is the inner sanctum of the soul. It is the sanctuary, so secret, of the spirit.

During a remarkable private discussion with the woman at the well, Christ stated plainly, "God is a Spirit: and they that worship him [i.e., pray to Him] must worship him in spirit and in truth" (John 4:24). This He said after carefully explaining to her that it was not some special geographical location that made it possible to meet the Most High in person.

No, indeed, if in truth we wish to have a close, firsthand encounter with our Father, the secret rendezvous is within our souls and within our spirits. This is the realm where He delights to reside, known only to us and to Him.

For the benefit of those who have only a vague, hazy idea of what is meant by the soul, the spirit, a brief explanation is helpful here. My book *Walking with God* deals with this subject in great detail.

A man or woman's soul is essentially his or her *person.* It has three distinct and remarkable capacities.

Emotions

With our emotions we act and interact with others around us, as well as with our environment. Our emotions influence our attitude and outlook.

Mind

Our remarkable capacity to reason, dream, learn, remember, and imagine comes from our mind.

Will

The innermost volition, which God's Word calls "the heart of man," the will, is the capacity to be so set and fixed on enduring decisions for good or evil that they determine our destiny.

This really is the innermost sanctum of the soul. It is essentially a very secret sanctuary.

Likewise the human spirit has three attributes with special capacities given to us by God, our Father.

Consciousness

Consciousness, sometimes called "self-consciousness," is that by which I am acutely aware that I am a unique individual who is quite different from all others. I also recognize that the universe is occupied by a supreme spirit—God the Father—whom I may or may not have met.

Conscience

The special capacity given by God Himself for me to "see," understand, and respond to His person and to

His presence is my conscience. With my conscience I can comprehend eternal truth. It is really my spiritual vision with which I can perceive spiritual realities.

Communion with the Most High

This is the capacity to pray—to "hear" God speak to me and for me in turn to speak to Him, in inner intimacy. At its best it is to be still, quiet, and at rest in His presence—knowing Him firsthand! seeking Him as He is! enjoying Him!

Christ assures us that in this same manner our Father "sees" the secrets of our hearts. He fully comprehends every detail of our inner lives. Only He understands every secret in our design. So He deals with us in utter integrity and total justice.

For you see, God our Father is here! He is not far out in space! He is present to hear me pray! He is here to reward my petitions!

Because of these truths I can pray in open honesty. I can pray in calm confidence knowing He hears me. I can pray without being phony in coming to Him as His child, assured He will answer in His own best way. This is the prayer of faith in God. This is, in truth, the way to pray. This in reality is to commune with God, my Father, in calm confidence.

There is a magnificent passage in Hebrews 11:5–6 where God's gracious Spirit assures us that this is the prayer of faith that pleases God. The prayer of faith actually blesses Him in a beautiful way. It satisfies His profound longing for intimate interaction with His children.

Our prayers in themselves are not great. It is much more important that He is our great, gracious God, who also delights to reward our prayers in wondrous ways of His own design.

He did this for Enoch who walked with Him in close communion for so many years. So it is possible for us, too, to please Him as we humbly trust Him from hour to hour.

This trust is best expressed as we open up our lives to Him each day. He should be given unimpeded access to every area of our affairs. We share every secret of our hopes, dreams, lives, and loves with Him. He should be granted open entry into every detail of our decisions as well as our daily duties. In short, He actually "shares" life with us while we in turn share in His abundant life. We drink of His life; we draw on His presence; we delight in His companionship. This is the essence of believing in Him. This is to truly know Him in reality. This is to be actually aware He is here.

And because of all His grace and goodness to us, we can be of good cheer. All is well within!

The remarkable results of this sort of prayer of faith are that He accomplishes much more in our little lives than merely answering our petitions. He actually changes and recreates our characters. From day to day His presence permeates our emotions, our minds, our wills. My soul is in fact conformed more and more to the likeness of Christ who becomes my dearest Friend. In His own gentle way His gracious Holy Spirit in power and peace sets my spirit free to see and know and follow God as my Father in profound loyalty. I learn to love, with deep devotion, He who first loved me long before I ever knew Him.

In this way I find it is a pleasure to pray. It is not a penance. Nor is it some sort of stilted, stiff performance. It is a profound, precious honor that I cherish in genuine gratitude. I can actually come to Him anytime, anywhere, for any reason. And if all is well I sense and know His warm welcome. So life with my Father is beautiful, beautiful!

For all of this to take place, allow me to urge you to take several sincere steps in your walk with Him. He will surprise you with joy.

1. In humility, earnestness, and contrition ask our Father to make Himself very real and dear to you. He will honor your prayer and draw near.
2. Honestly, openly admit your lack of faith in Him. Without flimflam or excuses, express your need to truly trust Him. You will be surprised how He responds.
3. Invite Him sincerely to enter your life—all of it— to share it with you. Also, ask Him to actually share His life with you. Ask that you can even exercise His own faith in you.
4. As He does this—and He will—thank Him. Thank Him! For He is your faithful, loving Father. You will begin to *know* His own abundant life!

2

The Prayer of
Honest Confession

From reading the first chapter about the prayer of faith, one might be lead to believe that such an intimate, close communion with our Father is constant. Certainly that is the deep desire of His own Spirit. And, likewise, it should be our deepest longing. But, sad to say, incidents do occur in our lives that interrupt the harmony between us, bringing great grief to Him and despair to us.

In His generosity and grace toward us He has made provision to mend the breach between us. He does not condemn us for our misdeeds but instead extends His gentle pardon. He does not cast us aside if we are prepared to admit our mistakes, confess our sins in genuine contrition, and turn in profound repentance from our wicked ways to seek His face and find consolation in His dear companionship again.

All of this is a most important aspect of the inner life

of prayer. It cannot be sidestepped, even though it may seem decidedly disagreeable to contemporary Christians. Our society, our culture, and our churches bend over backward to keep people comfortable. In fact the worldly skeptics sneer at God's people in contempt, claiming that all they desire is to be comfortable in their padded pews.

Still, Christ calls us to confess our iniquities, even if the church remains silent on the subject. The whole matter of profound repentance amongst God's people is not at all popular today, for it is bound to make people very uncomfortable.

John the Baptist preached repentance, Jesus the Christ preached repentance. The early church preached repentance. So must we!

Repentance and confession of our sins is not a simple, single, once-for-all action that takes place at conversion only. It is a profound process that occurs in a truly penitent soul that longs for close communion with God our Father.

In order to be both helpful and practical just here, it must be pointed out that if we truly love Him, if we are truly loyal to Him, if we are truly lowly before Him, we will not deliberately sin against our Father. We will not offend Christ our Friend. We will not grieve His gentle, gracious Spirit. Rather we will walk with Him in open honesty and sincere humility.

All of this is possible and entirely practical if we have and hold a proper view of God in all of His great mercy, His abundant generosity, His profound patience. We must also see His absolute integrity, His utter holiness, His amazing righteousness. And when we begin to truly grasp something of His glorious character, we will not sin against Him or others or even ourselves with impunity. We will not wink at our wrongs, brushing them aside as mere weaknesses. We will not treat with disdain or lightness our lapses in failing to honor Him, love Him, serve Him, and appreciate Him.

Again and again and again we must remind ourselves that not only is God the Most High our Father, Friend, and Fellow Companion—He is the Most High Majesty.

> He is the Eternal One.
>> He is Ruler of heaven and earth.
> He is King of kings.
>> He is Creator of all that is.
> He is the Supreme Judge of all.
>> He alone is our Savior.

Because of this we will see it as our humble duty and honest endeavor not to allow anything to intrude between Him and us. And if it does, we will be ready and willing to confess our sins and repent of our wrongs in profound remorse before Him.

Lest I be misunderstood here, allow me to repeat that it is not just because we have a sense of guilt that we come in penitence, but much more so out of a deep sense of sorrow, godly sorrow, for having grieved Him who is our Savior.

Again I remind you that confession of sin, profound remorse, and genuine repentance lead us into complete reconciliation. "If we confess our sins, he is faithful and just to forgive us our sins, and to cleanse us from all unrighteousness" (1 John 1:9).

He is our Savior! Bless His name forever!

He saves us from our past. He saves us from our guilt. He saves us from our sins. He saves us from the power of sin and death. He saves us from separation from our

Father. He saves us from Satan's deception. He saves us from our old self-life. He saves us from judgment. He saves us from hell. What a Savior!

A *savior* is a "deliverer." A *savior* is one who "sets you free" from your impossible dilemmas. This glorious Savior sets you free to follow Him in love and loyalty as His chosen child. Tragedy upon tragedy, sorrow upon sorrow, it often does not work out that way between us and Him. Let me explain why.

There are three tremendous adverse influences at work in every believer's life. Often, often they are not even recognized much less understood as being utterly abhorrent to God.

Pride

Human pride is the preeminent problem with humanity. Pride is the direct antithesis of the very character of the Most High who is so selfless, so self-giving, so willing to serve others. Our pride is an absolute affront to our Father. He declares emphatically that God resists the proud!

Yet we consider it quite appropriate to be proud of our civilization, our technology, our science, our affluence, our appearance, our careers, our families, our accomplishments, our personal charms, our sophistication. The list goes on and on. Then we wonder why our Father does not reward our prayers. We have become our own God—like the proud Pharisee who literally prayed with himself in an exalted sense of self-importance and self-righteousness. Read carefully and prayerfully Luke 18:1–13.

In those verses Christ commands us to pray all the time, but the prayer was to be one of profound penitence. The publican, so despised but humble in heart and contrite in spirit, was heard and rewarded.

Pollution

Most believers have no clear comprehension of how effectively the society and culture of which we are so proud has contaminated our souls and corrupted our spirits. Multitudes who claim to follow Christ really are friends to the world, far from our Father.

If we are ruthlessly honest with ourselves, we shall see that we have the same mind-set as the world around us. We have the same priorities, the same interests, and the same aspirations, the same attitudes, even the same lifestyle. Do we wonder then that God grieves?

Are we surprised to find trouble, turmoil, and tragedy intruding on our walk with our Father? Can two walk together unless they be agreed upon the enduring, eternal values of life? Bit by bit our paths separate. Our petitions go unanswered.

Perverseness

This is a double-pronged word that is used often in God's revelation to describe anyone who is (1) stubborn and self-willed, refusing to do God's good will and (2) resistant to God's clear commands, choosing not to believe His commitments or to act on them.

There are millions of people who know a great deal about the Bible. They study it, discuss it, love to listen to sermons about it—all as a purely academic exercise. But they refuse to obey it in humble submission to the Most High.

They will not come under the government of God. They will not give up their self-control to Christ. They will not submit to the guidance of His Spirit. In attitude and in action they are rebels in defiant opposition to God's splendid purposes for them as His children. Then they wonder why their prayers do not prevail. They wonder why there is no inner peace, no rest of soul.

From our Father's perspective, pride, pollution, and perverseness cry out for deep repentance. They cry out for the soul to be cleansed, to be changed, to be recreated in newness of life from Christ Himself!

If in deep conviction of soul you sense Christ's gracious Spirit calling you to deep contrition do not be afraid to respond in profound repentance. Cry out to God your Father to show you Himself! Entreat Him to reveal Himself to you in tender compassion and glorious grace. You will discover, as did Job, as did Isaiah, as did the sinners in Jesus' day, that He does not stand afar off as your judge. He does not remain aloof in cruel condemnation. He does not cast you aside. Rather He draws near to your broken heart (or will) to bind it up and reaches out His healing hands to touch and transform your contrite spirit.

That is the way to pray. That is what it means "to find His face" . . . "to come into His presence" . . . "to cry out Holy, Holy, Holy is my God." For in Him, and only in Him, is there healing for the soul, health for the spirit, wholeness for your entire life. Only He can make you wholly His own, and in that way, holy in life.

At the same time, in His infinite concern for you as His child, He will show you yourself as you really are. No longer will you indulge yourself in a proud, spurious self-image of superior self-righteousness. You will begin to see yourself as the sincere publican did. So humble yourself in godly remorse, to cry out from the depths "Oh, God be merciful to me a sinner"!

This is the earnest prayer of complete confession that our Father always hears and to which He always responds with complete forgiveness and total acceptance.

He rewards you abundantly with cleansing, consolation, and amazing changes in your character. His compassions fail not; His mercies are new every morning; His faithfulness is fresh and full just for you.

There is a word of caution that needs to be expressed here. Your confession of soul and spirit must be made to God Himself. It is against His goodness, His grace, His generosity that all of us sin so grievously. Only He knows all about you. Only He comprehends all the complexities of your convoluted character and conduct. Only He can deal with you in utter integrity, complete justice, and marvellous mercy! Only He can extend full forgiveness to you, utter acquittal for all your wrongs, and remarkable renewal.

No man, no woman, no pastor, no priest, no counsellor, no psychologist, no psychiatrist can accomplish this. Only Christ can! Only God our Father can fully accept you as His beloved child. Only His gentle Spirit can assure you all is well.

Several years ago a mature missionary, greatly used of God in central Africa, sat in our home and with utter sincerity told this moving story. She had been appointed to Uganda by her board. She had the idea she was God's special gift to the primitive people of that region. She came with enormous pride in her credentials, in her professional skills, in her personal expertise, in her own wide experience in education.

But God could not use her.

When she saw the open honesty of the African believers, their childlike confidence in Christ, their simple, quiet obedience to His bidding, she was broken before God. In godly sorrow she cried out to be humbled in heart (will) and mind and emotions. She called on Christ to cleanse and change and recreate her spirit before Him.

He did! He restored her. He renewed her.

From that time she has gone forth in wondrous ways to touch thousands of Africans with God's gentle grace—all because she humbly prayed the prayer of confession.

3

The Prayer of
Genuine Gratitude

The prayer of genuine gratitude might also be called the prayer of profound praise to the Most High. It is common in Christian communities to make a sharp distinction between prayer and praise. But across the long pilgrimage of my walk with God my Father, it has become abundantly clear that prayer and praise are in truth the two complimentary faces of the same coin. For without a deep sense of awe, wonder, gratitude, and thanksgiving to our living Lord, it is well nigh impossible to pray as we ought.

It is the person who really appreciates the honor of being allowed to enter freely and gladly into our Father's presence with honest humility who is heard. We each need to come often in this way not only to lay our petitions before Him, but also to lift our souls and spirits to Him in unabashed thanksgiving, gratitude, and adoration. We should thank Him not just for His blessings and benefits bestowed upon us, but more importantly, for the splendor and wonder of His own person.

The very character of Christ is of such a caliber that it elicits our deepest loyalty and our burning devotion. We must give expression in utter honesty to the greatness, the generosity, the goodness of our God. He expects this from His children. He is blessed and pleased and satisfied when we so honor Him.

It is noteworthy that many of us do this when things are going well. It is not at all uncommon to hear even casual Christians remark rather lightly, "Oh, isn't God good!" when everything falls into place. Or in a most offhand way they will say, "Someone upstairs sure takes care of me!" These are but examples of the rather detached and remote manner in which people give gratitude to God. It is almost as if He were their chore boy attending to their needs.

But for the seeking soul who truly longs to meet with our Father in profound prayer of genuine gratitude, no matter what life brings, there are powerful truths that must be learned from Christ Himself. These lessons come to us in times of trauma, turmoil, and tears of tough times. Only there do we begin to grasp God's ways with us. Only there do we stop our shallow pretence at praise. Only there do we learn the way to pray with gratitude when things appear to go very wrong.

As a young Christian, no single thing troubled me more than to hear people shout, "Praise the Lord. Bless His name, hallelujah!" when all was well in their affairs. Yet the very same individuals would give way to deep depression or dismay when things began to fall apart.

Then their comments were actual accusations against God. "I don't understand why He allows this to happen!

Has He abandoned me? Doesn't He realize what is happening? Does He even care? Where is He?" Across the long, long years of my life I have heard all the indictments. So it is for that reason I dare to write this chapter as I do. In essence it is a defense of God, both in what He always does for us and also in what He in turn expects of us as His children.

It is possible to pray the prayer of genuine gratitude to Him even in the greatest adversity. We can learn how to praise Him in absolute sincerity and integrity even at the worst of times. We can discover the secret of honest prayer and praise that releases His power to change us and to change circumstances amid any calamity. We can offer Him forthright thanksgiving in utter transparency.

Only in this way will we ever be changed from being *victims* of our circumstances to becoming *victors* in Christ Jesus!

Carefully read Philippians 4:4–7. This is a classic passage in God's Word that directs us clearly in the way to pray during times of difficulty. An explanation in contemporary terms will lead to a clearer understanding.

Rejoice in the Lord always (Phil. 4:4).

Here God's Spirit instructs us always to find our profound joy in the person of our living Lord, in His unchangeable character, in His enduring faithfulness, in His wondrous care, in His amazing grace, in His loving commitments to us, in His compassion that never fails.

He does not ask me to be happy at all times, for "happiness" is a human condition determined by what is "happening" around me. It fluctuates constantly in our affairs. My Father invites me to find deep joy, strength, serenity, and surety in Himself! Always these things are true praise.

Let your moderation be known to all men (v. 5).

This clear command implies much, much more than not overindulging in too much food, drink, or extravagant behavior. What we are told here is to live in quiet, gentle gracious ways amidst every adversity.

The outstanding hallmark of His follower is not only one of joy but also of quiet strength, calm serenity, and strong surety even in tough times. This is proof positive to everyone who is around us that our calm confidence is grounded in our God. A life of this caliber honors the Most High.

The Lord is at hand (v. 5).

Here is the supreme secret to the prayer of praise! I am acutely aware that always, always the living Lord is here. He is not a remote, distant deity. He is here.

> Jesus answered and said unto him, If a man love me, he will keep my words: and my Father will love him, and we will come unto him, and make our abode with him (John 14:23).

No other single, sure, unshakable reality in all of life can provide the Christian with such peace, such power, such praise. Christ's ironclad commitment to any person who loves Him and complies with His Word is that our Father will enfold him or her constantly in His love. Yet even over and beyond that, He our Father, Christ our Friend, and God the Holy Spirit will actually abide and reside with that person in constant communion.

Oh, what a noble honor! Oh, what a purifying impact on our little lives! Oh, how precious, how near, how dear! No need to fear! He is here ! So I can give Him genuine gratitude always!

Be careful for nothing (v. 6).

Sometimes this is stated as "be anxious about nothing," "simply do not worry," "be a carefree child of God." But so often the tragic truth is so much the opposite. When things appear to go wrong we fret, we fuss, we fear, we fume, we fight the adversity or fight others or even fight with our loving Father. It is a pathetic picture where fear replaces faith.

Again, let it be said here in tenderness: There is only one way to pray with praise amid all the darkness. Ask God Himself for the calm courage and strength of will to focus your attention upon His own presence with you. Cultivate His intimate companionship. He is here to help, to heal, to make you whole! All is well.

In every thing by prayer and . . . thanksgiving let your requests be made known unto God (v. 6).

Oh, so simple to say. Oh, so, so difficult to do! This must be, can only be, the action of God in my despair. He declares, "It is God which worketh in you both to will and to do of his good pleasure" (Phil. 2:13).

It is possible to pray with genuine gratitude under every circumstance in life. God does not mock us. He does not put us into the furnace of affliction to test our faith in Himself. My dear reader, He allows the tough times to come for two purposes:

1. To show us His amazing faithfulness to us in the furnace of our affliction;
2. To change and conform our own characters to His own.

Once we accept this tremendous truth we are undergirded with His peace.

And the peace of God, which passeth all understanding [and misunderstandings], shall keep your hearts [wills] and minds through Christ Jesus (v. 7).

No longer will we keep fussing and fretting and fuming. No longer will we keep on fighting the adversity; no longer will we keep arguing with our Father, protesting in dismay "I don't understand it!"

For in place of the fury, the frustration, and our false accusations against Him who cares for us will come His presence, His peace, His power to rest and repose in His utter faithfulness to me.

This is to then be able to pray with praise and in His power that changes everything, including me! Then I can truly bless the Lord with all my soul—even in deep distress.

All of this is possible for the person who has been born from above by God's own gracious Spirit; who humbly follows Christ the Lord in loving, implicit compliance with His commands; who in calm, childlike trust places quiet faith in God our Father to lead in paths of righteousness. Such a person lives a life of praise and honor.

When troubles come I can then wait quietly on God. He and He alone can sustain me in the storms of life. He does not forsake me. His noble commitment to me as ever of old is:

> Be strong and of a good courage; be not afraid, neither be thou dismayed: for the LORD thy God is with thee, whithersoever thou goest (Josh. 1:9).

It is not a question of being out of God's will just because things appear to go wrong. Rather it is to know His presence amid the storm, sustaining me in strength. This is of first importance!

Secondly, if I am living in harmony and goodwill with my Father, God, I shall not allow any sin to intrude or linger in my life. It will be confessed quickly. Then my conscience is clear. Then it is possible to see that any pain or problem comes only through His own gracious purposes for me as His child.

Oh, what rest and respite of soul He gives my spirit. Let me say it again. He is near. He is here. All is well!

Thirdly, there are times of trouble when I may feel my faith in my loving Father is too feeble. Fear not! Always it is His utter faithfulness to me that can preserve me from any peril, which can lead me in peace, which can deliver me from my distress—in His own wondrous ways.

My part is to wait quietly for Him in confidence. He will fulfill His noble purposes for my good!

Lastly, I need not be alarmed by the strategies of Satan. The Enemy cannot touch or harm or molest the child of God who abides in Christ. It is the presence of Christ, the power of Christ, the protection of Christ resident in me that preserves and delivers me from the Devil's devices.

> We know that anyone born of God does not continue to sin; the one who was born of God keeps him safe, and the evil one cannot harm him. We know that we are children of God, and that the whole world is under the control of the evil one. We know also that the son of God has come and has given us understanding, so that we may know him who is true, and we are in Him who is true—even in his Son Jesus Christ. He is the true God and eternal life (1 John 5:18–20 NIV).

Having explained the enormous part played by God in all the experiences of life, no matter what assails us, let me now point out our part in offering up to Him our prayer of praise. There are three actions of my will (or heart) involved. Here is a supreme secret to a life of victory in Christ.

1. In true humility and open honesty before Him, I acknowledge He is God, that He arranges all my affairs with only my best interests in mind, because He loves me. This applies even when things appear, to my view, to be awry.
2. Without opposing Him in the trial, I accept everything that happens along life's path as His provision. This is the path of peace.

    I do not fight life, trying in my own strength to change everything or everyone. They, instead, are quietly accepted and allowed to modify and mature me into Christ's own character.
3. In sincerity I actually approve of what God my Father does and how He decides to do it. This strong action, initiated by His presence at work within my life and soul, sets His gracious Spirit free to do abundantly more than I can ever hope or imagine.

    I praise Him joyfully, for it is He who is at work in me both to will and to do His good pleasure. This is to walk with God in peace, power, and praise. Then in all honor I can declare boldly,

> It is God who brought me here!
> It is God who can keep and sustain me here!
> It is God who will lead me on from here!

4

The Prayer of Relinquishment

Apart from the profound cry of confession, "Oh ,God be merciful to me a sinner," there is no other single cry of the sincere spirit and of the sincere soul to equal that of, "Oh, God, not my will but yours be done!"

This is sometimes called the prayer of utter submission to our Father's will for us. It is an action of the will that stands as a monument to the hour when a humble human soul in honesty relinquishes its rights to God Himself, for God to control his or her own life and do as He sees fit.

Christians across the centuries have given this deliberate action of a person's self-surrender to God various names. Here are a few:

- complete capitulation to Christ's control
- full surrender to God's sovereignty
- utter submission to our Father's will
- self-consecration to God's service

- losing one's life to save others
- letting go of one's rights in relinquishment
- doing God's will at any cost

In one way or another they represent the price one must pay to become the Master's follower. The cost is colossal! Few, few Christians choose to follow Christ in this way. The demands seem too drastic!

In our walk with God here on earth Jesus told us plainly very few would ever decide to tread this trail of tears in company with Him. Most people prefer to take the broad, easy, enticing road of self-service that ultimately ends in self-destruction.

> Enter ye in at the strait gate: for wide is the gate, and broad is the way, that leadeth to destruction, and many there be which go in thereat: because strait is the gate, and narrow is the way, which leadeth unto life, and few there be that find it. . . .
>
> Not every one that saith to unto me, Lord, Lord, shall enter into the kingdom of heaven; but he that doeth the will of my Father which is in heaven. Many will say to me in that day, Lord, Lord, have we not prophesied in thy name? and in thy name have cast out devils? and in thy name done many wonderful works? And then will I profess unto them, I never knew you: depart from me, ye that work iniquity (Matt. 7:13–14, 21–23).

So the prayer of self-relinquishment has two supreme purposes.

1. It is a full surrender of all my self-life, my self-interests, my life, my possessions, my future, to my Father God.
2. He can use this sacrifice to save others!

There is no other way in which to pray the prayer of total submission to our Father's sovereign will than that shown to us so vividly by Christ Himself in the Garden of Gethsemane. It was an ordeal of anguish. It was an act of eternal consequence whereby He chose not to save Himself in order to save others. No child of God can meditate over the momentous events of that night when Christ cried out in self-relinquishment, "Not as I will, but as thou wilt" and not be stirred to follow in His heroic steps.

But, but, the terrible tragedy is we do turn back. Most of us will not pay the price of self-relinquishment. At best we give mental assent and perchance even cry a few tears of emotional response to the cruelty of His crucifixion. Yet we will not deliberately, daily, with un-divided devotion take up our own cross in self-denial to follow our Savior, our Friend. Read prayerfully Luke 9:23–26:

> And he said to them all, If any man will come after me, let him deny himself, and take up his cross daily, and follow me. For whosoever will save his life shall lose it: but whosoever will lose his life for my sake, the same shall save it. For what is a man advantaged, if he gain the whole world, and lose himself, or be cast away? For whosoever shall be ashamed of me and of my words, of him shall the Son of man be ashamed, when he shall come in his own glory, and in his Father's, and of the holy angels.

Surely, surely, He has laid down His life for us. Are we then prepared to lay down our lives for Him?

For as we do, day by day, in the simple act of saying "No" to self, and "Yes" to Him, whatever is His will and purpose for us, He will then save others through our submission. There is no other way!

As we determine to do this out of love, gratitude, and honor for Him, we discover an amazing thing. He does not impoverish us. Instead, He accepts our sincere self-sacrifice with respect and joy. For now He sets me free— free from slavery to my little life—to enter fully into His own abundant life of adventure in His company.

In a few words, "What I give to God in mere spoon-fuls, He will return to me in shovelfuls of His grace and glory!" My life will be full, full. And others too will be free, free, saved from their sins to follow Christ.

Lest we should think the challenge of total self-relinquishment is too high a call for common people to accept, we do well to look at the lives of two ordinary men: Ornan of the Old Testament and Peter of the New Testament. Both demonstrate clearly what God can do with sincere souls prepared to pay the price of genuine self-denial.

In 1 Chronicles 21:18–30 it is recorded how King David had committed a grievous offense against the Most High. In pride and self-esteem he had ordered a military census to be made of the fighting men under his command, as if it was his military might and not God's power that had prevailed against his enemies.

The result was stern judgment fell upon him and his whole nation from the Most High. The destroying angel swept across the country leaving great casualties in his wake. Now suddenly the destroyer was poised over the city of Jerusalem itself, at the point of devastating the entire capital. How could it and its residents ever be saved?

David, in characteristic remorse and profound repentance for his own pride and folly, covered himself

in dust and ashes. Then he cried out to God for mercy
upon his perishing, stricken people.

He was ordered at once to offer a suitable sacrifice
for his sins on a special spot known just then as the
threshing floor (or place) of Ornan. It was the site over
which the angel of destruction hovered, having been
ordered to desist.

Ornan was a poor peasant farmer, not even an Israel-
ite but a remote remnant of the Jebusites who first built
Jerusalem. He had a wife and four sons, and they had
all fled in terror to hide when they saw the terrifying
angel over their poor, rocky, hillside farm.

Ornan himself, all covered in sweat, dust, and chaff
from the grain he was thrashing out with his oxen, was
approached by David, all covered in dust and ashes of
despair. David asked Ornan for his threshing floor as a
suitable site for the supreme sacrifice. He even offered
to purchase the spot. To us this seems simple. But not to
landowner's of those distant days. A man simply did
not part with property that had been held in the family
for hundreds of years, generation after generation. It
was his supreme security.

More than that, Ornan could have protested that this
land was the only way in which he could possibly provide a living for himself, his wife, and his four sons. It
was his life. It was all he had and knew how to do.

But there was no such debate from this dear man!
His prompt response stands as one the most noble ges-
tures of total relinquishment to God's will ever given
by a humble human being.

> Take whatever you see best!
> Take the threshing floor.

> Take my oxen as a sacrifice.
>   Take my wooden implements for fuel.
> Take my grain for an offering.
>   I give it all!

The last four words represent true relinquishment. Few, few, few of us ever utter them in honest prayer. We tremble at the cost. We will not let go of our control. We prefer to clutch our choices close to our own chests.

Ornan's amazing action was honored by God in wondrous ways. First, he was handsomely reimbursed by David for his generosity that saved all his neighbors. But in due time there was erected on that threshing floor Solomon's magnificent temple: the most majestic edifice ever built on planet Earth.

Turning our thoughts forward in time some 1,050 years, we find Christ at dawn on the shore of the lake of Galilee. It is after His resurrection. He has served His fisher friends a hearty breakfast prepared by His own hands. The little group sit around the dying embers of the little fire that warms them until the sun rises over their beloved lake.

How Peter loved the sound of the wavelets lapping on the shore. How he loved the fresh breeze off the water. How he loved the feel of a boat working beneath his bare feet. How he loved the strong tug of fish tangled in his nets. How he loved the banter with his buddies as they brought in a great catch. How he loved the barter and chatter that went on in selling the fish. How he loved his life as a rough and ready fisherman.

The Master had called him to relinquish it all. But, again and again, the old love and loyalty had drawn him back to his beloved lake. Once more on this calm dawn, Jesus looked at him lovingly and asked again and again, "Peter do you love me more than these?" It was a soul-piercing question. For, if he truly did, the cost of relinquishing them all would be colossal.

Peter that day determined to leave the lake behind. Like his Master, he set his face like a flint to go back to that terrible metropolis of murderers—Jerusalem—to live out a tempestuous life for the sake of saving others. He was prepared to give up his lake, his laughter, his love of fishing, his old life, to follow Christ in a cruel city that hated Him.

Out of this rough, tough fisherman's relinquishment and utter submission to God's will, more than three thousand people gave themselves to God in one day alone. And he himself became the fearless leader of the early church, with a flaming faith in the Most High. "*He is risen!*"

From the foregoing we can draw several divine principles that underlie the prayer of submission to God's will.

1. Total relinquishment frees us to truly follow Christ wherever He may chose to lead us. Only in this way is He in turn free to accomplish His own noble purposes in our little lives.

2. When in honesty we turn over all we are and have to His direction and control, we are no longer preoccupied with our self-interests. We are not busy covering all the bases in our personal affairs—we become expendable for Him.

3. Then, and only then, can He be given a chance to prove to us in poignant, practical ways that He can provide for us, protect us, empower us to do His will. What an impetus to our simple faith in Him!

4. Beyond even that, earnest submission to His control daily injects a brand-new dimension of delight into

our walk with Him. His buoyant, abundant life is injected into ours in amazing adventures.

5. Out of this enthusiasm (*entheo*—in God), for it is He who now works in us both to will and to do of His good pleasure, other lives around us are impacted. He actually works in us to bring people to Himself.

6. Through this intimate touch and great inner action of His precious presence within the sanctum of our souls and spirits, we are people of serenity and strength. Our complete confidence is in Christ! We repose in Him.

7. The ultimate end is that our characters and our daily conduct in His company bring Him deep satisfaction and joy. More than that, as His children, we bring Him tremendous honor. And we in turn are blessed, blessed—beyond our fondest dreams.

All this only became true and potent for me as a tough-willed man in midlife, when I fully capitulated to Christ. Let me tell just a little. Then you, dear reader, will realize that what I urge others to do is not mere doctrine or theology. Rather, the lessons were learned in the fiery crucible of my own anguish. They emerge from my personal response to Christ's call.

Until my early forties my first love was beautiful ranch land. I had owned and developed three magnificent country estates. The challenge of bringing these properties up to a high standard of productivity and beauty was really an all-consuming passion.

The broad expanses of my acreage were my love, my life, my interest, my expertise, my wealth, my pride, my privacy, my security, my fulfillment, my future security. In a word, I lived for land. It was my love.

Yet, in honesty, I declare here it never fully satisfied the deep inner yearning of my soul and spirit for the supreme meaning to my life. It was the false god that had usurped the place of preeminence in all my affairs. I was utterly blind to the deception I lived under.

Then one decisive day, amid my inner ennui and my desperate search to truly know the only true and living God, in His gentle way, He put His hand upon my land. Better to say, He placed His hand upon my hard heart (my stubborn will) and whispered softly, "Let go of your land. Give it all away. Come, follow Me!"

It was a traumatic time of soul searching. Oh, the awful agony of relinquishing all that had been my very life so long, the deep, deep decisions to submit myself and all I owned to the complete control of Christ, the terrifying intensity of turning over all of my future entirely to His will is beyond words to portray. But in His patient loving-kindness He showed me the way to pray in honest submission.

My life was transformed completely. He recreated me by His presence, His power, His peace. So now all is well and I am at rest as His child. I am satisfied!

5

The Prayer of Intercession

As we relinquish ourselves completely to Christ and to His purposes for us, He uses us to touch other lives. Where before we may have withdrawn ourselves from the sorrows, struggles, and suffering of a sin-stricken society, now we become engaged in it to save others. This does not imply we suddenly become so-called do-gooders, but it does mean we are a people of compassion, closely identified with our suffering Savior who weeps and works in a world gone wrong.

He Himself assured us this would be so.

> In the world ye shall have tribulation: but be of good cheer; I have overcome the world (John 16:33).

Much of the adversity we encounter will come from those close to us, with whom we interact often, yet who really do not know God our Father firsthand.

Christ Jesus warned us clearly, in Matthew 10, that some of our opponents may well be within our very own families. Some will be very self-righteous or so-called religious people, even within the church. Some may turn out to be friends who turn against us because we are loyal to the Lord God. Some may simply be individuals who hate and reject us without any good cause.

His clear command to us in every case is to

> Love your enemies, bless them that curse you, do good to them that hate you, and pray for them which despitefully use you, and persecute you (Matt. 5:44).

It is precisely at this point we must learn the way to pray for anyone whom His Spirit of love brings across the path of our lives. How do I intercede for them effectively?

A grand old man of faith once remarked to me: "Phillip, once you get to truly know the living Christ it is simple to trust Him for all your own needs in life. But it is a challenge of the highest order to exercise quiet, unshakable faith in Him for others in distress." Jesus Himself taught us clearly how to intercede in Luke 11:1–13. This is when His men asked Him to teach them how to pray as He did.

First of all He taught them the Lord's Prayer. I shall not elaborate on it here, for I have written an entire book on that theme. It is entitled *A Layman Looks at the Lord's Prayer* and can be readily obtained from any Christian bookstore or from many church or Christian school libraries.

Jesus then told the profound parable of the poor man who came to his friend at midnight begging for three small loaves of bread to serve an unexpected visitor. Most people in the Western world, with all our affluence and technology, have no idea of what this request involved.

Eastern hospitality demands that any visitor, traveller, or guest who comes to the door be invited in and served food. Obviously, by his own open admission, this man had nothing to set before his guest at this dark hour.

But, with boldness, he goes at once to his friend begging bread. This was no simple request, for his friend had already retired for the night with his family. So we must understand the sacrifice his friend made.

Poor people in Palestine lived in tiny, two-room hovels built of brick and clay. There was no electricity, no refrigeration, no central heating except a tiny dung or brushwood fire.

To prepare their bread, plain barley meal and water were mixed, patted out like a pancake, and roasted over the burning embers of the tiny fire. All over the East this is called *chapati*.

The neighbor friend protested because of the cold. He and all his family had climbed into bed together, cuddling up just to try and keep warm. The door was shut tight to keep out the cold. Now this knock on the door. Now this call for bread. Now this plea for help he could not deny.

He would rouse himself, search for a candle or tiny oil lamp to light the room, gather up a bit of kindling for the fire, all the time shaking and shivering in the chill night air. He would have to find flour and ice cold water, mix the two, then bake three little cakes of barley meal for his friend.

In every move he made there was suffering, suffering, and gracious self-sacrifice to meet the need of a neighbor. This parable is a poignant picture of our precise position when we come to Christ our Friend, knocking, asking, seeking help from Him for those who come to us in the dark hours of distress.

May I emphasize just here the exact cry that came. "I have nothing to set before him." That is an honest admission from an honest soul. The same identical cry for help should come from us when we go to Christ our Friend seeking help for others who turn to us in trouble.

Too long, for far too long, the self-assured, self-confident Christians of our contemporary churches have assumed their affluence, expertise, and modern technology could meet human needs.

They cannot. They do not. They will not. Only as we come to Christ in confidence, asking and asking; seeking and seeking; knocking and knocking, will He respond with His generosity, His compassion, and His resources to meet all our needs.

This is the way to pray in intercession for those who stumble into our lives in their darkness and despair. I do not have the answers or the resources for perishing people. But I have a Friend who does!

Robert Browning, the outstanding British poet, was asked near the end of his life, "What is the secret to your beautiful character and gracious conduct?" In quiet humility he whispered, "I have a Friend. His name is Jesus."

In essence, the living Lord Jesus Christ must ever be the one to whom we turn to find help, healing, and wholeness in our dark world, not just for our own deliverance, but also for all the other sad and weary travellers that come to our doors seeking some sort of sustenance.

He Himself went on to explain carefully, after concluding this parable, that we also must ask God, our loving, caring Father, to give us of His own gracious Spirit to succor us when others need help. It is the only way to pray in our times of turmoil.

Very gently Jesus pointed out that if a son should ask for bread, a human father supplies bread, not a stone. If the lad requests a fish for supper, he is not served a serpent. If he wants an egg, he is not given a scorpion!

We human parents do endeavor to supply the needs of our offspring with honesty and loving care. How much more, then, will our beloved Father God give us gladly the generous resources and gracious companionship of His gracious Spirit when we ask for His assistance?

Just as in the physical realm of our diets we need fresh food each day—fresh bread, fresh fish, fresh eggs—in the spiritual realm our souls and spirits need the fresh sustenance of God's own life. We must come to Him to find strength and satisfaction. We must partake of His life, of His Spirit, of His Word, for the words He speaks to us are spirit and life.

During the very intimate exchange that Christ had with His beloved men just before His own cruel death, He spoke openly about the great help His Spirit would bring to them. We need to understand clearly what He said.

> Howbeit when he, the Spirit of truth, is come, he will guide you into all truth: for he shall not speak of himself; but whatsoever he shall hear, that shall he speak: and he will shew you things to come. He shall glorify me: for he shall receive of mine, and shall shew it unto you. All things that the Father hath are mine: therefore said I, that he shall take of mine, and shall shew it unto you. . . . And in that day ye shall ask me nothing. Verily, verily, I say unto you, Whatsoever ye shall ask the Father in my name, he will give it you (John 16:13–15, 23).

1. He, the Holy Spirit, in response to our request for clear guidance, will reveal absolute truth to us, not only about our Father's desires in our decisions, but also about our own actions in assisting others. We are not wise enough to solve life's tangled troubles. He is! So we must act on the true solutions He provides. In a word, He will show us what to do.

2. Christ assures us that His Holy Spirit will in fact honor Christ Himself as He reveals to us that He is our Counselor. He is our Deliverer. He is our strength. Proof of this will be the gracious way in which He actually makes the life of Christ very real, very precious, very powerful to us in this time of need. He is alive. He is here. All is well.

3. Our Lord did His utmost to have all His followers understand that His Spirit did not come just to speak about God. Rather, our Father gives His Spirit to anyone who will ask for Him and will obey Him (Acts 5:32) in order to actually impart the very life of the risen, living, active Christ to us—daily. We partake of Him freely and afresh daily.

4. Christ goes on to assure all of us who truly follow Him and carry out His clear commands that our Father will honor our prayers of intercession. It is the way to pray in His noble name. In His own wondrous way, in His own appropriate time, for the ultimate good of those who love Him, He is able to make His grace abound in any situation! Bless Him!

If we turn our attention to the much beloved eighth chapter of Romans, we there discover explicit information on the way in which to pray in effective intercession. The gentle Spirit of Christ, who is the author of those pronouncements, reveals to us basic truths about our relationship to God in prayer.

He makes it clear that we must be lead and guided by Him. We simply dare not indulge our own desires, nor do we simply satisfy our own selfish instincts. On the contrary, our conduct is controlled by Christ, demonstrating to a skeptical society that we are the children of God.

In this honest, open behavior our Father is honored. Even more compelling is the inner confidence and unshakable assurance He gives us to call out boldly to Him, "Father, my Father!" knowing that He hears us.

In this same way, when I pray there is the strong, serene consolation that His Spirit imparts to my spirit that I am an heir to Him and a joint-heir to the living Christ, my dearest Friend. So we are all on the most intimate terms together in suffering for a perishing world.

Our intercession is not a solitary sort of activity in which we implore a distant deity to act on our behalf. Rather, God's gracious Spirit informs us explicitly that as part of God's family we are closely engaged in prayer together.

In fact as we beseech our Father to continually impart His Spirit to us, we find He actually prays on our behalf. Wonder of wonders! He knows all about our human limitations, our infirmities, our lack of complete understanding. We often do not know what to say or how to pray.

In our extremity, in our anguish, in the blindness of our burning tears, Christ's own sweet Spirit steps in to intercede for us with supernatural compassion and supplication, which cannot be uttered or expressed in human language. There is utter stillness. There is a sublime silence of awe upon the soul. There is an acute, intense awareness of Christ's presence as our Advocate pleading with our Father to reward the Spirit's intercession in His own wondrous way.

This is the way to pray in His Spirit. It is the way to pray in steadfast faith in God. It is the way to pray with confidence in Christ. For the initial impulse to intercede for others is actually formed in us by our Father who knows and understands us fully. As we struggle to give expression to the divine desire, we often stumble and stammer in the attempt. Then God's sweet Spirit, our Helper, our Alongside One, our Fellow Comrade comes to our aid and prays on our behalf according to God's good will.

Christ lifts these profound petitions to our Father, as our Friend, our Advocate, our Intercessor. All of it is accomplished in quiet faith, knowing that our Father will honor the endeavor in His own best way. He is the author of our prayer of faith. He is also the finisher of our faith so the intercession really begins and ends in Him!

When, in childlike trust, in loving obedience, in quiet confidence, we pray this way, we live to see that eventually, in our Father's good time, all things do work together for the ultimate benefit of those who honestly love God. Often this takes time, much time. But our Father is absolutely faithful to finish and fulfil the good work He begins in us. This is true of the prayer of intercession.

6

The Prayer of
Stillness Before God

In His love, mercy, and grace to us our Father God has provided three simple but sublime steps whereby we can come into close communion with Him. He longs for our intimate companionship as His children. He calls us to come to Him through Christ. Here are the steps:

1. He actually bestows on us His gift of faith so we can respond to the gentle overtures of His Holy Spirit, so we come to put our childlike trust in Christ our Savior, Friend, and Master.

2. Our Father also works in our little lives by His Spirit and through His own gracious Word so that we can comply with His will. Five minutes of obedience to His wishes will reveal to us more of His noble purposes for His people than five years of theology. Just do what He demands. You will be surprised!

3. He calls us to be still before Him. In this quiet
    expectancy, with humility of spirit and honesty of
    soul, we will discover He is very near to us.

This third discipline of soul does not sit well with our
noisy, strident society of the Western world. We are, for
the greater part, a people given to great activity, to sen-
sationalism, and to whatever is spectacular. This em-
phasis has spilled over into our churches from the
secular world. Still, God calls us to be still. Only a few
may respond. But oh, the wonder of quiet times in close
communion with the living Christ.

When He was here amongst us in human guise as
the Son of Man, Jesus of Nazareth, He was always slip-
ping away from His associates to be alone with His Father. He was never ashamed of these secret, silent
interludes of close communion. Nor should we be! Read
Mark 6:30–46.

There are seven special benefits that will come to anyone who will pray this way. They will help you come to
know God in a remarkable, precious way. They can
bring strength, serenity, and surety to your soul.

Stillness Before the Most High Is Creative

Almost anything God accomplishes is done in silence.
He does not, as a rule, indulge in noisy displays. Every
sunrise, every sunset, every flower bud bursting into
bloom, every blade of grass emerging from a seed does
so in silence.

All the finest inspiration (breathed into people by His
Spirit)—whether in art, music, literature, science, or
spiritual life—takes place in the stillness of His presence. It is not created in confusion, chaos, and the clamor
of our creative activity.

It is in the serene stillness of His profound presence that we sense our souls become serene. There we find rest, repose, and re-creation. Only in intimate and first-hand interaction with His Spirit am I remade in His likeness. Christ's own superb character impacts mine. I become like the one with whom I spend My most special time—daily.

One Must Be Still to Hear God Our Father

To hear God implies three personal responses on my part:

1. I recognize in truth it is Him speaking to me;
2. I ready myself to respond in faith to what He says;
3. I actually, then, resolve to go out and do His bidding.

Most of us are so preoccupied pouring out our own petitions we will not pause to listen to what He tells us. Be still. Be calm. Be receptive. Wait confidently for Him to instruct and guide in the way He wishes you to live. This is the way to pray.

Our Father has chosen several specific ways in which to commune with His own beloved children. It is essential to understand these. Then life with Him becomes a great adventure as we learn daily to carry out His wishes and bring enormous pleasure to Him.

1. He speaks clearly to us through His own Word. Read it. Ruminate on it. Reflect on it. Resolve to act on it in faith.
2. He speaks to us through the remarkable life of Christ. It is He who is the visible expression of the invisible God.

3. He speaks to us through the still, small, inner voice of His own Spirit. He convicts us in how we ought to live.
4. He speaks to us through the splendor, design, order, and beauty of His created world. Spend time outdoors alone with Him.

Be Still and Wait on God to Act in His Own Time

We of the Western world are impatient people. We want instant action. We demand a quick fix. We insist on immediate results.

The terrible truth is we treat our Father in the same way. That is not the way to pray!

We must mature and learn to wait calmly, patiently, for Him to carry out His own good intentions toward us in His time and in the manner of His own wise choice.

We are a generation on the go . . . go . . . go. We are people who rush . . . rush . . . rush. We are busy . . . busy . . . busy. No wonder individuals wear out, burn out, and break down!

Christ, just as with His own disciples in His earthly days, calls us to come to the awareness we need to be still. We need to get alone with Him. We need to sense the still, refreshing dews of His presence, His peace, His power to restore our souls and spirits. Give Him time to do this!

To do this in a practical way, find a quiet spot where you can have a secret rendezvous with God. Set aside a special time to be alone with Christ in close communion. Compose your soul calmly. Quiet your emotions, concentrate your mind on your heavenly Father's great generosity to you to allow His Spirit to speak to your innermost heart (or will), from and by His Word.

You will be refreshed. He will not disappoint you.

Your spirit will be serene. Your soul will be at rest. You will be strong in your confidence in Christ. Then you can calmly go out into the weary world knowing God will use you to touch others with His own divine love and dignity.

Be Still and Watch Him Work in the World

We live in drastic days of dreadful degradation. Our once-Christian civilization has despised and rejected Christ just as deliberately as did the society of Jesus' day. At that time, He warned of dreadful, divine judgment that would fall on Jerusalem because of it. It did! The history of Jerusalem's total destruction by the Romans can make your blood run cold. The unbridled slaughter of over a million Jews and their crucifixion on countless crosses is almost beyond comprehension.

It is time contemporary Christians woke up to the terrible terror of cataclysmic judgment, which will consume our world unless people repent. In stillness and in solitude Christ can convey to us clearly the supreme perspective that He has of human affairs. It will change our cozy complacency. It will drive us to our knees in honest intercession for a perishing world plunging into perdition. In stillness we must watch for God to redeem His world.

Our Father yearns for His children to awake to the fact we need His might to make things right. For far too long we assumed it was our skills, our plans, our programs that would turn back the tide of evil sweeping over society. Only He can, by the majestic power of His own supernatural Spirit!

In stillness, in solitude, in sincerity there are those stalwarts who in severe self-sacrifice pray and pray and pray for a mighty quickening of Christians across the earth. It is a high calling to stand strong in unshakable faith and see what great things our God can do in a world on the edge of anarchy and utter destruction. This is a solitary, unsung labor of love.

In Stillness Christ Draws Very Near

It is essential for us to understand clearly that our Father is not only delighted to have us draw near to Him in quiet communion, but He in turn loves to draw near to us. He loves to make Himself known in reality to His child. He revels in the company of the one who is humble in heart (will, soul) and contrite in spirit.

> It is in stillness we bare our souls before Him.
> In solitude we honestly confess our sinister sins.
> In silence we wait to hear Him speak peace.
> In serenity He assures us all is well.

At such times we sense and know and repose in Christ's precious presence. His profound peace flows into our spirits. We are renewed with His power to face the day and all its demands.

God's gracious Spirit bears quiet witness within my seeking spirit that He is here! He is near! He is very dear! And because of Him all is well!

This is the way to pray in privacy and in purity. Nothing is hidden. All is open. Hope comes anew.

> It is He who wipes away the tears of our inner anguish.
> It is He who speaks consolation to our contrition.
> It is He who heals our wounded spirits.
> He gives us the joy of gladness again.
> He it is who re-creates us.

For the seeking soul, the hours of stillness and of

solitude with the living Christ become treasured times. I urge you, get to truly know God this way.

Be Still and Honestly Worship the Most High

Perhaps there is no other encounter with our Father that leads us into utter humility and quiet brokenness before Him. In solitude we sense something of the supreme purity of His person. We are still, subdued, in awe and wonder at His absolute holiness.

Like Isaiah of old we are overwhelmed with an acute awareness that we are people of profane lips and wayward wills. Yet Christ comes to us with those endearing, nail-pierced hands to touch our sin-stained souls. He brings healing to our sorrowing spirits. He brushes away the hot, burning tears from our flushed cheeks aflame with shame as we whisper in hushed tones, "Holy. Holy. Holy!"

There sweeps over us, around us, through us, an amazing awareness of indescribable delight of wholeness.

I am forgiven.
I am cleansed.
I am re-created.
I am made new.

This generates such an upswelling of gratitude, praise, and worship that it flows from us freely, spontaneously. This is true worship, honest worship at its loftiest and most noble level. His Spirit injects into our spirits a new dimension of strength, serenity, and surety in Christ.

It is out of such remarkable moments that I can go out into our sin-stained society and boldly, gladly, gratefully speak of our beloved Lord—without shame and without apology. For He has met me. He has touched me. He has made me whole!

It is all His grace, His generosity, His goodness. So I am glad, glad, glad to go on His behalf.

In Stillness Christ Fills Me with His Spirit

> In the last day, that great day of the feast, Jesus stood and cried, saying, If any man thirst, let him come unto me, and drink. He that believeth on me, as the scripture hath said, out of his belly shall flow rivers of living water (But this spake He of the Spirit, which they that believe on him should receive: for the Holy Ghost was not yet given; because that Jesus was not yet glorified.) (John 7:37–39).

Oh, the wonder of just coming to Christ in open, honest, and deep longing to be refreshed with His life! He invites us to come day after day to drink and drink of Him. There is no other way to pray and to ask to be filled and filled and filled, again and again and again.

If I am to be fit and healthy and strong in body I must drink fresh, clean, pure water day after day. If I am to be strong, buoyant, and serene in spirit I must drink anew of Christ's Spirit and life day after day. Then, and only then, can there flow from my own innermost being rivers of His living water to refresh others.

Just outside my office window, about a hundred yards away, a glorious mountain river leaps into life with rushing rapids from the great, still, deep lake above it. Often, often, I stand in silence at the torrent's edge and in quiet awe watch the clear, cool water of the lake fill and fill the stream channel with its power. Life, energy, refreshment, beauty pour moment by moment out of the deep still lake to fill and fill the lovely river flowing by my door.

Christ tells us it is exactly the same with us. We are but the channels through which He can pour the power and refreshment of His own life. In stillness we repose in Him, open to His presence, allowing Him to fill us constantly!

7

The Prayer of Patience

Even for the most consecrated Christian, there are times of trouble, of tears, of turmoil when *it seems God is silent.* Those five fallible words are put in italics on purpose. From our purely human perspective there are dark, difficult days that we sometimes call the "winter of the soul." Prayers, no matter how honest and sincere they may be, remain unrewarded, and in our sincere distress we wonder why our Father does not respond.

It is imperative that this issue should be discussed openly in a book of this kind, for learning to pray in patience, with complete confidence in Christ, is one of the supreme secrets to finding renewed strength in the Most High. It is the one way to pray that brings serenity and surety to our spirits amid prolonged adversity.

In order to understand how to pray in patience, it is first of all important to point out the errors many of us make when things appear to go very wrong. This is not to be demeaning to the person who is impatient, but rather to show the folly of our fickle attempts to resolve our dilemmas and untangle our own troubles.

I write these lines as a most solemn warning. For I have struggled and struggled in my own willfulness to do what only God can do amid the darkness. These pages come out of the pathos and pain of my own pilgrimage. And they come with compassion and deep concern to anyone who treads the valley of tears.

The first thing we do is *worry* when there is delay. Somehow we assume we can fret or fume or even fuss our way out of the situation. It really does not work and only wears us out emotionally.

Secondly, if that strategy does not succeed, we really do go to *work* on the knotty problem. We throw our thoughts, time, and energy into the dilemma. We will work it out!

More often than not the end result is even greater complications, with ever deeper dismay.

Thirdly, in our extremity we will decide to *wrestle* with God over the matter. In our folly and in our frustration we feel sure we have good reason to accuse Him of neglect. Does He not hear our pleas for help? Does He not see our sorrow? Does He not care for us amid the downdrafts of our darkness and despair?

So the struggle of soul goes on within us. It takes a terrible toll not only of our mental and emotional strength, but also of our spiritual confidence in Christ.

For those of us who have been nurtured and taught in the worldly ways of the Western world, three basic behavior patterns help to explain our conduct in crisis. It is most important to understand these concepts so we can learn to pray in patience.

Impatience

We really are people who not only want, but often demand, instant action, immediate results. We will not endure delay. We are brought up that way. It must happen today.

Our whole mind-set is one of getting things done in the shortest time possible. So we put ourselves and those around us under constant pressure to perform.

This leads to continual stress and tension, one of the most destructive forces in our lives and families. It does great damage to our serenity of soul.

Sad to say, the same impatience spills over into our most precious relationship with God our Father. We not only expect instant replies to our prayers, but also demand that He act at once on our behalf. We will not wait!

Impetuousness

Our Western world is exceedingly complex and complicated because we are such ingenious people. If one idea will not work at once we immediately turn to another. This principle applies to every area of life, be it science, technology, education, commerce, or Christianity.

With our impetuous drives, we dash from one extreme to another. We take off on tangents without weighing the consequences. The total end result is chaos and confusion in our culture. We are attracted by anything new or novel as long as it works, though it often works to our own ultimate ruin.

As a people we are the same in our association with Christ. It is increasingly rare to find those who have complete confidence in Him, who are doggedly loyal to His clear commands, who will exercise implicit faith in Him when their little world has gone wrong.

Importance

We feel so important, so self-assured, so smart, we insist on taking full control of all our activities. All around us we see the wreckage and waste in the lives of people who demand the right to make their own decisions even when they lead to self-destruction.

It is not much different for many who claim to be lead by God's gracious Spirit. They actually refuse to obey Him or His Word of divine insight. They will not submit to His direction.

Then, if the events of life go awry, they will not wait on God's good pleasure nor on His time. They choose rather to seize control of their own conduct and decide to do their own thing. This is dangerous. For God will give you what you demand!

His Word gives tragic accounts of His people insisting on getting what they wanted, only to be ruined by it:

1. The nation of Israel demanded meat from God in the wilderness. He sent them great flocks of quail to eat. Not only did they endure awful physical suffering, but also languished with leanness in their souls.
2. The same sort of terrible thing happened when later Israel demanded a king from God. They got Saul, a cruel tyrant. There was only trouble, trouble, in the nation.
3. King Hezekiah, when smitten with terminal illness, turned his face to the wall and demanded divine healing. His life was extended long enough for him to know that his children would be enslaved, his nation invaded, and God's temple plundered.

Still most of us will not pray in patience. We will not

wait for God's good and proper time. We will not trust Him in childlike faith to simply work out His solutions in the dark days.

I was one of those people.
I write from the pain of firsthand anguish.
I know what it is to worry, to work, to wrestle.
It took a dark, desperate, discouraging interlude in my
    life to learn how to pray with patience; how to wait
    quietly for Him to reward my earnest pleas; how to
    find new hope, life, and joy emerge from the storm.
To tell of it briefly here is to bare my soul. But I dare to
    do so in the assurance Christ will use it to save some
    out of great distress when things look so dark.
It is possible to be patient in prayer.
It is possible to honestly wait on God.
It is possible to rest on His strength and utter
Faithfulness, amid the storms of life!

As a young man I searched for and finally found a chunk of land by the sea where I could develop a fine ranch. It was the embodiment of so many of my dreams. It had nearly two miles of lovely shoreline, open meadows with gorgeous old oaks, glorious views over the ocean to the snowy mountains beyond. I thought I was set for life!

But there were to be dark, dark days ahead on that spot we called Fairwinds. There would be some terrible times, even though I loved the land with a passion and worked strenuously to succeed.

First I began to lose my sheep to cougars.

Then the lambs died in fierce storms and from poisonous weeds. No one seemed to know why.

About this time my wife was stricken with cancer.

Then one dreadful day, government agents came to our cottage door to announce all our land was being expropriated for a naval installation.

All of my dreams were demolished! Utter darkness descended. And the gloom deepened into despair as we waited month after month after month for any money so we could even make a move—not even knowing where to go.

I confess openly I really did not know how to cope. I had worried and worried. I had worked and worked. I had wrestled and wrestled with God and with others, all to no avail. It seemed no answers came. Only silence.

Then one dull, dreary day, with a severe winter storm drenching the ranch, I noticed for the first time several big bald eagles perched serenely in a big fir snag by the beach. They just sat there resting, not concerned, waiting out the weather.

In an instance of spiritual illumination I was made aware: "They that wait upon the Lord shall renew their strength; they shall mount up with wings as eagles."

There was the key. There was the way to pray in patience. There was the time to just wait on God.

The eagles simply rested, relaxed, and restored their strength while waiting for the sun to break from behind the clouds. Warm thermal updrafts would build over the land. In renewed vigor they would stretch their wings, mount high on the rising air currents, and soar again against the sky.

If they could do this in calmness, so could I! Quietly, I, too, would wait for my Father, at work behind the clouds, to warm my world with His presence and His power. Again I would sense the upsurge of His Spirit lifting me above the storm damage. Once more Christ in His infinite compassion and mercy, new every morning, would open up great new vistas of life and joy and adventure for me, borne up, up, up upon His eternal faithfulness. He did just that! And it was then I began to truly wait on God. Then I learned a little of praying in patience.

To understand clearly what all this means to us, read prayerfully Lamentations 3:17–26. It is a tremendous insight into the wormwood and the gall that this noble man of God, Jeremiah, had endured. Yet in His mercy, compassion, and utter faithfulness, the Most High had delivered him into new hope and abundant life.

It is not always easy to wait for God. But it is the way to pray and to find rest in Him

May I assure you He is ever at work behind the scenes; He never does desist. As you trust Him, gently He will in due course show Himself in His mercy.

Then it is you must respond surely to His Spirit. In open faith spread yourself and soar up in thanks.

Give Him your hearty thanks in open praise. And give Him your humble trust—in simple prayer. These are the two wings with which you mount up above the obstacles of life. With your confidence in Christ you triumph over trouble. The wind of His splendid Spirit can lift you to new heights of joyous adventure with God.

For all of this to happen there are several very practical steps to take that can please and honor our Father as He strengthens us in the storms.

1. In honest humility come to Christ day by day. Cultivate His companionship as your dearest Friend. In genuine sincerity ask Him for His very life to be imparted to you. Only with His grace, His patience, His quiet strength can you possibly wait calmly for

God to work things out. He will! And you will find rest.

2. Make it a habit to remind yourself of His unfailing faithfulness to you in the past. Thank Him for His compassion toward you as a person, which never changes. Be oh, so grateful for His mercies which come to you afresh each day.

3. Do not forget to thank Christ, too, for His generous gift of faith that enables you to truly trust Him in the tough times. Ask Him to increase your capacity to rely on Him, to rest in Him even during the darkest hours. He will honor you for this.

4. Pray for His perspective on life amid all your perplexity. Let His gracious Spirit show you plainly that in your pain you are also becoming a nobler person. You are being transformed from character to character into the very likeness of Christ your Friend.

This is the way to pray in patience. And it is the way to wait on God in quiet hope.

Other Books by W. Phillip Keller

God Is My Delight
W. Phillip Keller examines his own personal relationship with the Trinity—God the Father, God the Son, and God the Holy Spirit—and shares his insights with those who are on the same journey he has traveled. Keller will give the reader a deeper desire to know God as Father, the Son as Friend, and the Holy Spirit as Counselor.
3051-8   256 pp.

Joshua: Mighty Warrior and Man of Faith
W. Phillip Keller, author of *A Shepherd Looks at Psalm 23,* provides an interesting look at the successor to Moses and conqueror of Canaan. Keller examines the man and mission and gives practical insights for those in the Christian battle.
2999-4   184 pp.

Outdoor Moments with God
W. Phillip Keller gives an intimate and deeply spiritual recounting of moments spent with the Master—working in the yard, hiking in the mountains, or simply surveying some magnificent expanse of land and sky.
2996-x   192 pp.

Sky Edge: Mountaintop Meditations
Out of the depths of his own heart, W. Phillip Keller shares with his readers insightful meditations from his mountaintop experiences illustrated with his own beautiful line drawings that convey in visual form these beautiful mountaintop places.
3052-6   208 pp.

Songs of My Soul: Daily Devotions from the Writings of Phillip Keller, compiled by Al Bryant

Excerpts from W. Phillip Keller's many books are compiled into a beautiful daily devotional that displays both the grandeur and goodness of God and our spiritual riches in Christ.

2995-1   256 pp.

Strength of Soul: The Sacred Use of Time

Strength of soul and serenity of spirit are the vistas Phillip Keller opens to his readers in this wise, perceptive look at what it means to live a full, rewarding life not only in one's retirement years but throughout life.

2997-8   216 pp.

Triumph Against Trouble: Finding God's Power in Life's Problems

Can God be trusted to handle the worst of things—in His way and in His timing? Out of difficult circumstances, W. Phillip Keller shares some of his most personal and encouraging reflections.

2994-3   144 pp.

Wonder O' the Wind

In this companion volume to the popular spiritual biography *God Is My Delight*, W. Phillip Keller relives his trek back to Africa and eventually around the world in the Lord's service.

2998-6   244 pp.